# Granite Facts

**CALUMET EDITIONS**
Minneapolis

Second Edition December 2022
*Granite Facts*. Copyright © 2022 by June Elizabeth Skjervold.
All rights reserved.

No parts of this book may be used or reproduced by any means, graphic, electronic, or mechanical, including photocopying, recording, taping or by any information storage retrieval system, without the written permission of the publisher except in the case of brief quotations embodied in critical articles and reviews.

10 9 8 7 6 5 4 3 2

ISBN: 978-1-959770-45-9

Cover and book design by Gary Lindberg

# Granite Facts

## Collected Poems and a Short Story

## June E. Lobdell-Skjervold

CALUMET
EDITIONS
Minneapolis

To everyday poets

# Contents

## PART I

Confession of the Romantic . . . . . . . . . . . . . . . . . . . . . . . . . . 3
The Source of Summer . . . . . . . . . . . . . . . . . . . . . . . . . . . . . . 4
The Tree Fort . . . . . . . . . . . . . . . . . . . . . . . . . . . . . . . . . . . . . 5
The Cardinal . . . . . . . . . . . . . . . . . . . . . . . . . . . . . . . . . . . . . . 6
Vacation Snapshot . . . . . . . . . . . . . . . . . . . . . . . . . . . . . . . . . 7
Wander Wind . . . . . . . . . . . . . . . . . . . . . . . . . . . . . . . . . . . . . 8
Milkweed Pods . . . . . . . . . . . . . . . . . . . . . . . . . . . . . . . . . . . . 9

## PART II

Into the Sun . . . . . . . . . . . . . . . . . . . . . . . . . . . . . . . . . . . . . 13
The Last Word of Summer . . . . . . . . . . . . . . . . . . . . . . . . . 14
Someday . . . . . . . . . . . . . . . . . . . . . . . . . . . . . . . . . . . . . . . 15
Let pass another day . . . . . . . . . . . . . . . . . . . . . . . . . . . . . . 16
Some Day . . . . . . . . . . . . . . . . . . . . . . . . . . . . . . . . . . . . . . 17
A Silvered Tree . . . . . . . . . . . . . . . . . . . . . . . . . . . . . . . . . . 18
Regrets . . . . . . . . . . . . . . . . . . . . . . . . . . . . . . . . . . . . . . . . 20
The Long, Long Grass . . . . . . . . . . . . . . . . . . . . . . . . . . . . 22
Wisdom . . . . . . . . . . . . . . . . . . . . . . . . . . . . . . . . . . . . . . . 23
Beyond Forgetting . . . . . . . . . . . . . . . . . . . . . . . . . . . . . . . 24
The Moon's Vanity . . . . . . . . . . . . . . . . . . . . . . . . . . . . . . 25
For Love of the Sun . . . . . . . . . . . . . . . . . . . . . . . . . . . . . . 26

The Oriole.................................................27
Alone ....................................................86
Flower...................................................97

## PART III

Relics on a Gothic Building ............................33
I. .......................................................34
II. ......................................................34
April Lament.............................................35
Ghostly Echoes ..........................................36
Math.....................................................37
Shallow Generations .....................................38
Dissertation.............................................39

## PART IV

Courage .................................................43
Darkness.................................................44
The Road I Walked .......................................45
The Sacrifice ...........................................46
Lassitude................................................47
For Love of the Sun the Moon Went Down ..................48
Winter Wind..............................................49
Remembrance and Forgetting ..............................50
The Nature of Time ......................................51
Pear Blossoms ...........................................52
Evening..................................................53
Frailties - Soliloquy I .................................54

Soliloquy II . . . . . . . . . . . . . . . . . . . . . . . . . . . . . . . . . . . . . . . . . 55

## PART V

Fragments . . . . . . . . . . . . . . . . . . . . . . . . . . . . . . . . . . . . . . . . . 59
How Long the Heart's Mourning? . . . . . . . . . . . . . . . . . . . . . . 64
Step High over the Wet Grass . . . . . . . . . . . . . . . . . . . . . . . . . 65
On the Exactions of Ezra . . . . . . . . . . . . . . . . . . . . . . . . . . . . . 66
The Song of Summer . . . . . . . . . . . . . . . . . . . . . . . . . . . . . . . . 67

## PART VI

On the Impossibility of Reconstructing a Past . . . . . . . . . . . . . . . 71
Then and Now . . . . . . . . . . . . . . . . . . . . . . . . . . . . . . . . . . . . . 72
Winter Song . . . . . . . . . . . . . . . . . . . . . . . . . . . . . . . . . . . . . . . 73
One Round and Turning Year . . . . . . . . . . . . . . . . . . . . . . . . . 74
Time Gone . . . . . . . . . . . . . . . . . . . . . . . . . . . . . . . . . . . . . . . . 76
Stone . . . . . . . . . . . . . . . . . . . . . . . . . . . . . . . . . . . . . . . . . . . . 78
Wander-Wind . . . . . . . . . . . . . . . . . . . . . . . . . . . . . . . . . . . . . 79
Alibi . . . . . . . . . . . . . . . . . . . . . . . . . . . . . . . . . . . . . . . . . . . . . 80
Untitled . . . . . . . . . . . . . . . . . . . . . . . . . . . . . . . . . . . . . . . . . . 81
Harlequin Charlatan . . . . . . . . . . . . . . . . . . . . . . . . . . . . . . . . 82
My Dancing Days . . . . . . . . . . . . . . . . . . . . . . . . . . . . . . . . . . 83

# Part I

# Confession of the Romantic

At last I know the great mistake
That led me where the false gods love to sing,
When I slept beneath the silver poplar tree
    to a delicate disturbance of its leaves
And watched against the spectacle of sky
    its lonely line,
And carried in the mind such promises
The child I was has never changed its age
Still knowing how it slept
Beneath the silver poplar tree

Only now I see this great mistake
Later years do not efface
But one that taunts me in its summer grace
To try to tell what never may be told

And why should I conjecture unto death
Translations of a theme as slight as wind
    passing through the silver poplar leaves
And why should I with madness in the corner of my eye,
Run despairing circles round the stars
    chasing my echoed cry…

June E. Lobdell-Skjervold

# The Source of Summer

      How was she to know
      Summer eats its joy
      Out of the hand that's young
      And will not come again
      To recognize the debt
Such days deceived even the time-wary mind:
No one could have told
How many had been squandered
or how many more
remained to drift across the lawns,
and warm the cellars and the homes of mice,
city alleys, and the stones around the lake,
or hang their dripping shadows over long and quiet roads
ending in inviolable secrecy about the source of summer
and of the love she spun within that time abandoned time
How was she to predict
how the heart is eaten from the spring born birds
and the same summer
will not look again
into the hollow nest

# The Tree Fort

Wind stirs the tree fort the children built
with no roof to shelter their dreams
— only dancing stars through the leaves
    at night
Now and then they return to that airy place
held fast by the willing branches,
to lie again in their castle rooms.
A different wind now brings
October flight from a season
past remembrance, past regret.

June E. Lobdell-Skjervold

# The Cardinal

Brighter than any berry of the fields,
I see the Cardinal among
ragged weeds
now and then
on these cast-off days
quietly feeding in the tangled growth
as though exiled from
some fine garden
with his queen, they illuminate
a somber scene

# Vacation Snapshot

There we stand by the sea
Smiling like guilty children
At our brash cleverness
having escaped you, Time,
O witch of the World.
There we stood once by the sea
and were captured, though not quite caught
at the nearly perfect crime


Now that you're gone

June E. Lobdell-Skjervold

# Wander Wind

The last penny of a meager patience spent,
time has been waited out,
one day your absence will fill the room.
See by the blue-green eye of the cat
they are diving for pearls
from the clean warm rocks.
By that blue-green eye they need you
to find the greatest.
Or by the white hair on this old man's head
They are daring your mountain.
Slept in the bitter snow
of a winter-covered country
no towns defy.
By the grey stare of certain streets
they are selling flowers from the corners
in a city so amazed on hills
the people there must laugh to climb them.
And by the dust on well-known books,
the too familiar stairway,
some inner thaw unbinds your will,
wearies the feet of their unvaried steps;
let them go.
Out-waited patience is a dangerous virtue:
yours is a civilization
rooms cannot contain for long.

# Milkweed Pods

Months now, I've studied from the window
some milkweed pods
like frozen captured birds,
clinging to their fragile stalks
adrift in the snow.
Small sentinels, they quiver in the wind
but do not break.
Somehow they've endured
fed this fancy and magic to an inmate's eye
Only rain can bring them down
with other elegant designs of dead vegetation;
Only the persistent rain
can break their spell and mine, perhaps.
Locked away in my memory
is an upstairs bedroom, a half-forgotten vision
of bright sunlight on faded wallpaper
and from the window, raged sounds
of ice and snow falling down,
haphazard channels running away with the road.
Revelations in the ragged yard, and
winter's myth exploding all around.
One was not safe in an upstairs bedroom
alone with the terrible, undoing spring.

# Part II

# Into the Sun

Winter's parole now broken
I'm released out of doors.
Unaccustomed to strong light,
among wonders of clay pots
garden hose and a remarkable spade.
Blinking and vulnerable I climb aboard
this one-way afternoon
heading into the sun my source
from which all lessons grow
straight into the sun
clay pot that I am.

The question is how
to keep time with time that will not be
kept track of, after all…
memories that will not…
Give me this day the right of way
bordered with red geraniums that shall endure.

June E. Lobdell-Skjervold

# The Last Word of Summer

The last word of summer has been said
and heard by the sudden yellow ash tree,
the slower buzzing flies,
by a clan of blackbirds
who reached the conclusion out of sky
to join forces and move on
While we gather our rightful Gold.
Gathering song of fools, they sing,
Move on before the plundering wind
but it troubles the undecided
at what strange tree they will
celebrate arrival.
I have to know a destination when I go.
Besides, I have forgotten how to fly
(a small matter in times like these).
Though the urge to soar still struggles,
Bird within us echoing the call,
this much I know,
though desire haunt the undecided mind,
birds may flee, summer insects die
the scarlet sumac burn too fast
and the ground soon bares itself to the
silent, impersonal snow…
I shall stay

# Someday

What shall I say to you in the language of some day…
    Light green "perhaps"
    Shining yellow "possibilities"
    Deep violet words of "waiting"
All colors of some day
Spoken with smiles to pretend a future
And when you forget
And I have outgrown hope
We shall move in the abiding grey.

June E. Lobdell-Skjervold

# Let pass another day

I cannot write about love today
Come back when I have earned my years
Autumn wise, and I will tell
How in that seasonless time
Silently, I learned I could not tell my love
And cannot tell it now,
The stars and tears too near the eyes
That saw love born in an earth of certainties.

Love chose with me brief shelter here
And left a dream the touch I do not dare
Or up a careless image
Will gather out of the air it must rejoin
And will occasionally look at me.

This silence overtakes with a stealthy grace
And stops before my eyes
Fancy, trailing its children of colored wishes
That do not make my heart a quiet place;
Let pass another day to weaken love's necessity.

# Some Day

Again some day
you will come
Reminding my world
Of what it may never attain
Again some day
Into the disbelief
On what I live by
With sure insight
Into this vague absolute of art
you will come
With your smile
At the sad knowledge
you are not real

June E. Lobdell-Skjervold

# A Silvered Tree

"And took a mess of shadows for its meat…" (Yeats)

Stands a question in the night,
my love, put by shadows
that have crossed my steps
a thousand times; my steps that lead
round the sleeping blocks of houses to pause
where the street lamp silvers a tree.

Complicating the sidewalk, are the shadows
of the many branches silvered on the tree
silvered by a street lamp ringed with night,
a Wonder, that has made me pause
and think on my unquiet steps
or why to you, they do not lead.

Steps that to you will never lead
find beneath a silvered tree their pause
where stands a question in the night
in the form of this unearthly tree:
Whether love with its unearthly steps
has taken me beyond return to its own land of shadows…

## Granite Facts

Stands the question in the night,
my love, a night of early summer shadows,
night of gentle death for those who will not want another
                                              —night of pause;
for I have newly learned how human steps
beyond their human power sometimes lead
and cannot follow past a corner street lamp challenging a tree.

How shall I call the night,
being earth-bound creature not designed to live with shadows?
How shall I call a love that does not lead
Where others walk with certain steps?
And how shall I forget how I did pause
and see these questions in a silvered tree…

For those who will not hope again, well is the night,
but to find implied intentions in the shadows
means betrayal if they do not lead
past morning's first light on the steps
where the shadows crossed and I was lost to pause
for you, and find my love said by a silvered tree.

Stands a tree that is a question in the night,
though morning shall erase the steps that lead
to that indifferent land where pause the shadows.

# Regrets

    The large snow
    easy falling,
    vanishes soft
    like individual regrets
    into the pavement…
And out of its fascination comes
the gloom of slush in a city street
reminding my human eyes of the fabled good and evil,
inviting me to laugh down the beggared streets,
sing a song or
dance about the circumstances
that felled the town of Troy.
Pagan reverence give O to the burning sun-shield,
proud guilt in the sky
    after all the white beauty
    is deceived
    to the earth…
Boast loud the triumph
of evil air in the streets;
our clerical coats worn thin,
rejoice, why not in the kinship
that makes soldier-clerks of us all
and expand the disproved soul by a laugh
long with the gods of hate;

Granite Facts

for the glory of a false nation-sun,
    a fever in the sky,
        will not fall easy
        like the victim snow
        mingling with these regrets.

June E. Lobdell-Skjervold

# The Long, Long Grass

Feet running swiftly
through the long, long grass
Changing sharp direction
now and again
Remind me of despair
through the young, young grass
and among Spring pear trees
under an evening colored sky.
Mad feet
wronging the hillside with distress!
What vast indifference
of a hillside
for the slim human folly lodged in you,
forcing you swiftly
through the long, long grass

# Wisdom

When you chose the wisdom
of shutting out all the street dust
inseparable from human relations and cares,
devoting to the mind's perfection
all your days;
And I chose to see I could not choose,
but become some discarded thing,
A white nightshirt hung upon a clothesline
Ghostly in the dark,
Silly by day in the wind's distortion,
When you chose the wisdom
of renouncing me.

June E. Lobdell-Skjervold

# Beyond Forgetting

Nothing can undeceive me now,
so inextricable my thoughts become
with the visible wind
and the sound of passing shadows.
Your sustaining food
dissolves without taste
I claim no appetite
for brief historical nourishment,
but shall keep with briefer fictions.
One admonition if you would call me back;
to fill my own vacancy
is contradiction.
You must be past remembrance
— I am beyond forgetting
and all things
that attempt to undeceive me.

# The Moon's Vanity

In the beauty you wear
    how much of subtle care is there,
Moon, of a still-born summer night?

Did you meditate this high success
    over the earth or only guess
That such an elusive light would go well
    against black-decorated night?

How much deliberation in the way you stood
    between those two and made them stay
A sympathy each away; those two
    who presumed to prolong a moment of moon,
Two children enamored of indifferent beauty
    that might if it cared eternalize their own.

So seemed to say the moon to them that still they stood
    and let slip each the other's heart
Until they moved content to dream apart.

How much design of witchery, I ask the moon,
Give you claim to trail the curious prize,
On a still-born summer night when you rise.
Two loves human pledged to the moon?

June E. Lobdell-Skjervold

# For Love of the Sun

For the love of the sun the moon went down
Slid the crown from royal night
While crowds of stars burned on
Till they too slowly paled from sight
and for love of the moon went out.

Fairy tales are for believers
and your kids won't for a minute

# The Oriole

Oriole is back today
I cannot see him
but sweetly from a nearby tree
comes his particular song.
I know he has a birds eye view of me
If I could I'd give to him
some sign of welcome
and my heart-felt wishes
for his summer sojourn here
but I am mute compared with him
to greet that herald as he greets me.

# Alone

Something about the quiet darkness making the scene obscure
And in the cool, tasteful air
That hints revelation of a secret—without ever revealing.

Something about the water catching moonlight on its cellophane surface
And in the faintly stirring trees remotely mournful
That excites a desire to have the secret, know the answer
Something, something I cannot discover, understand.

Always wanting, needing the meaning above and outside;
Always reaching out frightfully intense for assurance of it
Then the knowing it does not exist...

Visions of empty worlds, feelings of being alone in space
Feelings of aloneness resembling some opaque substance
Yet not like the substance of darkness blotting out the known and real

Disturbances of the soul—Do they ever resolve into peace?
An aloneness I cannot accept, understand.

Balancing it on our brain we shall bring back to you
—The Holy Grail, filled from the Fountain of Youth with the potion of Truth

# Flower

Soiled, parched flower,
Why do you stare at eternity—
Why pretend you don't know about me?

# Part III

# Relics on a Gothic Building

I will take my comfort
      with the blue stone angels
           who have heard great music
and are silent;
      in a blue stone solitude
           they wait again
                above my space of time
                      on the green earth.

Looking up at them
      I have felt contempt
           for their dumb detachment…
Now I take my comfort with the four stone angels
      in their blue medieval chill;
           four attitudes of reverence
                towards the sky.

June E. Lobdell-Skjervold

## I.

Reconcile us with the morning;
Night cause great rebellion
against the pain of remembrance forming
Out of facts collected under the sun;
Collected and paraded restlessly
As though some order might be found in that sea.

This new grey light now comes too soon
upon that injured dream of time
and its recall in the night,
A space of sleep away, that unsolved yesterday.
Reconcile us with the morning
Sung by a summer sun too soon.

## II.

Yet whom do we propitiate
Out of the orderless sea,
The god of a childhood gone,
The mind's church is an altarless place…

# April lament

I lied
        when I denied April's cruelty
When I looked up and boldly said:
"This is no season to lament!"

I lied
        and breathed too deeply of the air…
A mocking-blue sky heard my defiance
And afterward
The young wind kissed my forehead…

How cruel of April,
        engaged in all the insurrections of a Spring
        to countermand the orders on my heart
And bless the love
suffered an April ago

I would not have had it freed,
for the sake of neutrality in a perilous season
But emotion escaped with the tyrant month.
Now, the outcast stars and I
watch destruction in the name of April
        wild with new memories upon
        recognizing an old victim.

June E. Lobdell-Skjervold

# Ghostly Echoes

Most haunted of all my native road's memories,
    a low, dark structure, fierce in moonlight,
described around with skeletal trees and banked with snow
    disturbed my reconnoiter along quiet ways
known in childhood for their antique, unchanging quiet.

The grown stranger stopped and became
    native child again, unnerved by possibilities
arising from the pointed emptiness of a place
    man built to enclose his troublesome spirit
and the native child ran from its fascination
    While the grown stranger speculates

On his biographical road and the record
    of a shabby religious past
Resurrected every Sunday by a violating
    tribe, deaf to ghostly echoes.

# Math

      Incontrovertible
      as arithmetic,
With variations on a numerical imagination,
      The forms
      make one equation,
      Arrangement
      being irrelevant
      as an ice cream cone
In school they seldom doubt what the teacher says
Nor do they think too much
      Which accounts
      perhaps
For the amazing variations
      numerical
      In the jig
—Incontrovertibly—
      To the grave
      as arithmetic

June E. Lobdell-Skjervold

# Shallow Generations

Chimes shrill the air
Sounding shallowness of generations,
Prevailing noon with pangs of courtesy
as I climb the stone steps

This learning falters
Confronted with its own reflection
of a sterile life
And pangs of courtesy impinge a supplication:

I would this hunger
bend my knee
to the shallow generations
While the air shrills
Over stone steps at noon

# Wind

Blow the leaves less gently
Sympathize the sun less warm
upon the image of a white square house
Stop the birds
these things conceal,
delay sentence passed
not by wind or sun
forget mercy of shadows
upon an unreality of street
or human artifice
Death, do not notice
where life has failed
These things conceal,
delay sentence passed
not by death or shadows.
But particularly,
for the sake of tawdry leaves
and other reasons
Blow the wind less gently.

June E. Lobdell-Skjervold

# Dissertation

At least
there is bread in the house
and milk for the cat

twin consolations
behind a window open to a city

energetic with importance
ending in admission

behind an open window
a vacancy of interest
in this splendid search

while stumble on the floor
dreams all the bread in a house will not feed
crippling one who entertains
cold speculation

the cat will never know
tucked in itself, greedily curious,
never know,
who has milk for imagination,
how dreams are fed,
but then
obviously, through the open window
we also live by bread

# Part IV

# Courage

Courage is a fragile thing
Cradled in the strong arms of my hypocrisy
And all day I marvel how weak this ill constructed thing
Were it not borne in the strong arms of hypocrisy
Surely it would break a thousand times
This fragile thing speaks good meanings
Comments on the weather
Gives its routine of smiles and firm expressions
Looks stupidity in the eye
Walks over the mud and climbs the stone stairs of the moon
Makes its way like a mole through the crowds
Opens books, empties ash trays, even performs with dishes
And most astonishing of all
Meets your face, hears your voice
With ordinary signs of recognition
Yet when I close my door at night
When there is no more world but me
The strong arms of hypocrisy must collapse
I know so well the fragility of this poor thing courage

June E. Lobdell-Skjervold

# Darkness

As a child
I was afraid in the dark
Sometimes afraid in the dark

Now I am humbly grateful
Grateful for the invention of night
And sometimes fear
The dark will never come

# The Road I Walked

Wind that drives the human to his shelter,
Pity me.
The rain has lost its memory
And washes endlessly the pains of earth
brought back to life.
And all I was and would have been escapes me now
but faintly pushes at my mind as
the same road I walked, I walk again
Where is the link between that time and this?
Only in the sense of trees
heavy with rain
Returning sharply in the knowledge of this place
where I also possess and am possessed.

June E. Lobdell-Skjervold

# The Sacrifice

Something creates two words,
Divides two worlds,
and calls them past and future;
Something that is the present.
Two ideas
of all past knowing and future being
divided by an unfixed point in consciousness
demanding the sacrifice
of one world to the other…
Bury half of all awareness
Amputate one leg of time

Mind held in stasis or
distorted equilibrium
by its two dimensions,

Let the blade of this moment decide

# Lassitude

With a certainty
ill-timed
I find my will appropriated;
Something sleeps my energies that
they will not move a mind,
dissuade the eyes
from a truth
told by cracked places in the ceiling
of a room, or world
— Categories emptied of their definitions
exact words fail
and I cannot tell
Ceiling from cracked sky—
It is all ill-timed
devil of reflection
resting in my bones
appropriating
my world's youth
in an ancient room

June E. Lobdell-Skjervold

# For Love of the Sun the Moon Went Down

For the love of the sun the moon went down,
Slid the crown from the royal night;
I saw the stars wander naked and pale
Till they too slowly slipped from sight
And for the love of the moon, went out.

Vanity! My sullen tongue decreed,
the world aches its chain of vanities
Whole celestial wisdom is contained
in the vanity of the moon and stars.

I thought the issue loud and spent the day
recording what I'd seen, resigned to folly
When all at once the light upon my paper changed
And last I wrote the words:
For the love of the moon, the sun went down.

Ah the secret of the smiling desert sphinx
Yet I have told to the sad simplified words
To a careless disbelieving crowd
Out of ancient vanity the world spins on.

# Winter Wind

The wind, the wind was fresh against her face
and she was sad;
Fresh and damp against her face and yet so old
the wind that crossed the moors that winter,
finding her again many years away
alone on a different ground…

I felt the wind and thought it sad
Remembering unbent hopes we spoke once
now melted from us in the teacups of an afternoon.
So think the wind has found you not alone;
though blowing fresh and mocking free,
it flutters gently ancient memory.

June E. Lobdell-Skjervold

# Remembrance and Forgetting

Some brightly audacious notes
    each one an instant color of delight
Burst into this room
and filled it with gay, ethereal melody
that did not belong here
    in this room

I asked what should be done
with this fairy-light joy of sound
that threatened to distract my soul

Bury it temporarily under some well-remembered stone
    bury it well

And like the three spring crocus
    yearning from a glass prison on the desk
Those crystal notes
    a happiness of sounds
that threatened to distract my soul
Are buried under a well-remembered stone
    are buried well
Many days away lies the time
when I shall be reconciled
to the silence of this music

# The Nature of time

The importance of days, jerkily interwoven with nights,
will be secondary
when I reach the time of knowing
this music can never be played

Many days from this one
shall bring the acceptance of this cold cloud of fancy
reminding me that a fondness for music
not to be heard
will pass.

Yet I am plucked back by each day
measured into the hope
for the sound of this music.

Reality of one fancy will not be exchanged
for the truth of another.

Why am I condemned to know
the nature of a time
many days away…

June E. Lobdell-Skjervold

# Pear Blossoms

In that time, pear blooms were squandered on the trees,
I remember, making earth magic and a myth
I could not sing the praise of, or the gift.
Young was the color of the grass and sky;
young was I to grieve apart
for brief blossoms appointed to sift
Down around the ruins of myself, the profligate.
Schooled not to squander;
the profligate's assertion overcome,
all is remembrance of how I should have been
Arms filled with pear blossoms
who might have gone on to discover
how dreams are said to another
unwiser lover under the charms of that time.

# Evening

I left the week unfinished in my room
Deserting many things that caused the dull defeat
Of a conscience twice betrayed within a week,
And walked away past clocks and
Obligations, leaving them marooned;
Those same sane demons that would have me keep
Exhausting imitation of the frightened human sheep
Who dare not shut away in rooms their doom.

I stepped into that space before night
When children troop home and the city is concerned
To light itself against a deepened sky;
And on my fugitive flight I think I learned
How peace may be described upon a height
Of vigilance for the young who must be returned.

June E. Lobdell-Skjervold

# Frailties - Soliloquy I

      I tell you
      the Hand unjust
      that fitted into man
      a sense of grief
And left him
      half-grown in mind
      to reason out
      all heaven's frailties.
With some, the pain will not be localized
      but looks out of each event
      in life and nature
      as the monster
            Truth.
These push their shadows every morning
      through the streets of Hell
For every error of the beasts;
          each mistaken wind
      that rides men simply
          as wild ducks;
      or (especially)
      the glimpse of passing sky in frequent places
      under foot when defiled winter melts,
      and in the eyes of lovers;
All contain a link to personal woe,
      vibrating misplaced grief
      at heaven's frailties.

# Soliloquy II

I tell you
the Hand unjust
that fitted into man
a sense of grief and left him
half-grown in mind to reason out
all of heaven's frailties.

# Part V

June E. Lobdell-Skjervold

# Fragments

I

Interrupting a thought…
Halfway up the stairs…
Before the first note touches the next…
In a quick glace thru the open window…
all that lies forgotten by the present
looks at me.
For time is careless of the past,
burying moments
hastily before they die.

II

Cry crimson cat
the red wine weak with tears.
No bread but the red painted bread box
All – objects, among
      scattered thoughts on the table.
      Courage! brown cup,
love saw its image,
Still, no cheese
creep cat down the crafty back stairs.

What can be said now
in the silence after music…
Vague sunlight of tomorrow
curls the tender page
where I have written to the moon.

I am no more
identity lost before found
on point of—
One moment more…
But something,
necessity to translate,
gets in the way

Dark,
soothing a soot in the brain
day made,
Reminds the wound of kindness
no words intercept
dark at emotion's source
LET US HAVE NO MORE LIGHT!

Granite Facts

## VI

Waiting for things to pass,
the dead to bury the dead
that never die,
Wait till earth
trades with sky…
for this thing to end,
Sterner fate never was
than waiting infinitely
for a finite, dimensional end

## VII

Out of suffering, wisdom they have said,
gleaned from books
with a logic second hand
For such knowledge I have gained
will not record itself in books,
all absence of logic
in unending of logic
in unending tears
that admit no understanding but the washing of a pain
Whose companion
the raving of the mad wind

## VIII

       This One
escaped in the afternoon
into private exhilaration and was
free, under the comic, afternoon rainclouds
to contemplate the quickly speckled sidewalk,
Sudden freedom bringing
spontaneous knowledge
to one, alone in the afternoon
      of unplanned rebellion
          and mock storm
              brief as freedom

## IX

A lovely ghost
converts days to uncompleted dreams
moving within
to rhythm of contradiction,
Mocking decrees of banishment,
this loveliest ghost,
Deriding fears that it may be
unintentionally forgot
or that at some point
farther on
It will be more than ghost

My destiny being a mist of mistakes
I am content to make,
Futile is the warning
Of one calm, prophetic moment
When resolution
Forbade me dream again

Misled by fancies over-lapping
purple sky,
grass-green waters,
love that measures every step,
Is to walk in paths
of gorgeous stupidity

June E. Lobdell-Skjervold

# How Long the Heart's Mourning?

How long the heart's mourning?
Long, long the heart's mourning

No time like two years, seven days
length of its bereavement

Long, long the bright color of its agony
worn as inward show of grief

No official land of the dead
where the living may lament, consoled

Long, long the mourning…
Denied its own existence

Only in the larger sorrow of a kitten
leaping at the moon's shadows

Find the heart's long mourning

Granite Facts

# Step High Over the Wet Grass

Step high over the wet grass
      bringing your foot down quietly
      that you do not disturb the blades
      loaded and ready to spill magic water.
Walk cautiously about the edges
      of the sudden abysses in the sidewalk
      where the sky secrets charm you
      into the depth of danger.
Remember you promised to keep your feet dry
      — condition you eagerly accepted
      for possession of a morning
      that had dawned only for you
In the days when days dawned only for you.

Step high that you do not cause
      the blade of grass to spill their magic water
      Nor disturb the calm sky secrets that
      patch the sidewalk with mystery
Remember these things now that mornings
      have slipped out of your possession
And no more conditions restrict you – but one.

Remember these things as an antidote for the
grain of time-sand caught fast in your eyes

June E. Lobdell-Skjervold

# On the Exactions of Ezra

Dedicated to June Lobdell who cannot have it because I know she does not want it. (Unknown author)

Pondering a blank page
After you, my pompous Pound,
Have unsaid all the things
That to poets are so sweet
Is rather like
Stepping on a cold-and-very-damp-wash cloth
With warm and unsuspecting feet.

# The Song of Summer

The song of summer ends
by some neglected pond
where Autumn writes the trees in crazy scrawls
startling this believer in Summer.

Into the new silence
fall so many yellow leaves
I grieve for what once grew green
and the long, soft grass
I grieve for the long soft grass
and what once grew green.

# Part VI

# On the Impossibility of Reconstructing a Past

There was a green, pale lady
a lady all in green
passing under three trees
three bare and formal trees.
Touches imagination
this pale green lady
with a coldness
like the snow
and wishes me forgotten.
Slender and all in green
her foot disdains the dance;
Remembering words will not stray the gaze
of a lady green
passing under trees
three bare and formal trees
leaving with me
a coldness
like the snow.

June E. Lobdell-Skjervold

# Then and Now

Now it seems
they laugh
at poets who have written out their lives
in grief
over an unlived happiness,
an unsuccessful love.
There's a mighty contrast
between the time of Wyatt
and the time of now,
it seems,
when poets must speak
like Cassandra,
in grief, yes
but not over merely the metaphorical heart.
It seems…
But I am not amused
with this now archaic theme
and could find tears
for a poet's love gone wrong

# Winter Song

A wanton weather sits upon the hill
and you and I, pale exiles,
stumble through our sleep
as who should find the keeper of the snow
to make our peace with him upon the hill…

Though I plead death to end all things,
you should ask where the wild strawberry grows
perfect in the shade and be shown
the meaning of the reachless summer sky.

A wanton weather sits upon the hill
and whips the dreaming trees
unpitied by a frozen moon.

June E. Lobdell-Skjervold

# One Round and Turning Year

One round year beyond particular chaos
debates achievement…
Who will buy the past?
Memory culls with no mercy
      the images folded,
           rounded,
rolled into one year ago and
Time-gone skulks in the belly of today.

The architecture reappears
of faces and shirts they wore;
of incidental statuary
in the shapes of little girls
who swung red-handled jump ropes
one round and turning year ago
who wait around the corner
in your evening stroll
poised to shatter poise
the force that broke their red lollypop
on the objective sidewalk,
Raising distraction where the tears were made
and fell all rashly into chaos;
Raising out of this more careful ground
where strangers stand,
the same wild harvest.

## Granite Facts

But never whisper to polite groups
      how red lollypops break
           loud advice,
Time-gone practice to surprise the eyes
with exact pictures of the meanings
by which we tell our years.

This day too that harmless slides
along, a grey cat going to join grey cats
as you stroll home
cuts no sense of loss
But will surely come again
waking out of time gone
That in some unappointed hour
There will be known about the padded feet
Their marvelous, capable claws.

June E. Lobdell-Skjervold

# Time Gone

One year round beyond the source of tears
does not—
      (you know)
is hardly compensation,
Memory culls with no mercy
the images folded,
rounded, rolled into one year ago and
time-gone skulks in the belly of today.
Though you would not be traditional
the architecture reappears
of faces and the shirts they wore,
And even skinny little girls,
with red handled jump ropes tied in the middle,
passed miles ago,
wait poised around the next corner,
in your evening stroll,
Poised to shatter poise,
like the force that broke the red lollypop
on the objective sidewalk,
and damn the place where tears were made,
    and fell,
Raising out of this more careful ground where strangers
stand,
the same wild harvest.

## Granite Facts

But never whisper to polite groups
how red lollypops break
into loud advice:
Time-gone practices well to surprise the eyes
with exact pictures of the meanings
by which we tell our years.

This day too that harmless slides
along, a grey cat going to join grey cats
as you stroll home
cuts no sense of loss
But will surely come again
     waking out of time gone
And in some unappointed hour
There will be known about the padded feet
Their marvelous, capable claws.

June E. Lobdell-Skjervold

# Stone

Roller-skating children scream by on the afternoon sidewalk
    warmer inside than the pale afternoon light
And their shadows swiftly brush the stone
    concealing so well a dream
The pale light vanishes into pale grey rain
That forms a dull glaze over this stone
    and cannot reach what is hidden underneath

# Wander-Wind

Grant leave of absence
To one
  On the heels of a wander-wind
    A conscience's sickly wars
      have tired him out
        Ask no charities of him
          to build your church
      Leave him off the soldier list
        dedicated to your country's strength
      Consider him no prospect
        for a daughter's security
    Laws follow him
      lost hell deep
        To a conviction
          Tied to the heels of a wander-wind
         that once only
            tenderly touched the cheek

June E. Lobdell-Skjervold

# Alibi

That human life goes on
In the face of a prevalent attitude
that it might as well not,
Is, when you stop to consider,
somewhat amazing

But also proof of a delightful discrepancy
Between thought and actions
Without which there would likely be
no alibi called human nature

# Untitled

The rain pounding wails outside
Seems to have caught the rhythm
Of the music I am playing inside

June E. Lobdell-Skjervold

# Harlequin Charlatan

On a winters day
Four crows share a branch
high in an oak
like portents of an event
only they can see.
Snow sifts down.
I cannot shift my vision
to a gentler time;
It's much too cold.

# My Dancing Days

Miss Laurie looked out to see how the auditorium was filling up and after a minute or so, noted with satisfaction everyone was turning out in spite of the cold night. They always did for Miss Laurie's Christmas concert and there probably would be a certain number without seats having to stand up in the back. The place was noisy now with people settling in their seats, taking off heavy coats, greeting their neighbors and with kids running up and down the aisles. Soon the room would be quiet; quieter than it was for any other occasion. Every year Miss Laurie held her audience almost breathless and felt for the group a sympathy she could never bring herself towards its individual members. Her eyes shone as they always did when she was deeply moved or excited. Perhaps her success with the students was partly due to her expressive eyes that communicated beyond her words the mystery of the music she wanted them to feel.

For three months Miss Laurie worked with a group of students ranging from freshmen to seniors, practicing during lunch periods and after school. During the last weeks they had come back to practice at night, singing with their coats in the chilly auditorium for an imagined audience. Miss Laurie had had to campaign for her Christmas concert since the high school supported no regular glee club. After the first few successful experiments, her old students invariably returned with new recruits. Miss Laurie never worried about available talent and rarely had to turn away a student for total lack of singing voice. Usually, she could make anyone sing who came to her through making him want desperately to sing. Experience had convinced her most of the young had voices useful in harmony once they were properly motivated and taught. The task she set herself was difficult enough along with teaching her English classes but Miss Laurie worked with an unfailing inspiration. Aside from loving and knowing a great deal about music in general, she had a special belief about the Christmas music: that Christmas was to be found in the music of the carols, was the sum of attitudes and associations translated by that music. Miss Laurie herself couldn't sing except to carry a tune and played the piano with the necessary minimum of skill but she worked from her belief which was part pagan theory, formulated long ago, and part emotional intuition, as she would have termed it. After Christmas, the group never sang until the next year, no one being able to induce the English teacher to step out of her role and coach them in other songs; she always refused with some excuse.

Miss Laurie turned to face the group assembling on the stage behind the curtain. She automatically tucked the back of her blouse into her skirt and smoothed her black hair; there were more grey streaks in it, Miss Laurie had noticed tonight. Her eyes shone with an extraordinary brilliance, returning a youthfulness to her face she wasn't quite sure she had ever had. A few of her students who had never before been aware of anything about Miss Laurie except her rigid height, were amazed to see in her now a kind of beauty. Before she left the stage, Miss Laurie had some last minute instruction and encouragement to give. She looked about to make sure everything was in order. The backdrop looked fine: a monk's cloth drapery on which was painted in black outline, the great door of a cathedral. Large wooden steps led up from three directions, these occupying the stage itself. Artificial snow, liberally sprinkled over the steps, glinted in the focus of the footlights. Miss Laurie had instructed the boys to wear their brightly colored flannel shirts and dark trousers, if they owned them—overalls, even. She looked particularly now, at the shoes of some of the boys who she knew helped with the evening milking. The girls had made long, full skirts of solid color, wearing around their blouses, dark blue kerchiefs or shawls. They took their places now on the steps of the "cathedral", arranging themselves in various groups rather than rows. Miss Laurie smiled:

"I doubt that you resemble any group that ever stood on the steps of a cathedral. But I myself am extremely pleased with the way you look. It's color we want. Christmas is gay; pathetically gay and colorful, as you know by now the Christmas music is. Most of you have been to Minneapolis recently to see the gaiety there." Miss Laurie was interrupted by mirthful acknowledgment. "I missed most of you last Saturday night for practice, I seem to recall. Nicollet Avenue is very lovely, isn't it, and on each lovely corner people willing to shiver all day long, ringing bells for the Salvation Army. Christmas is like that. It dances in thin clothes and in warm robes. It talks a little sadly about joy and love, and joyfully, boldly rings the bells of its own doom. But it sings and dances to the last."

Miss Laurie had talked quietly but vehemently and now she saw by all eyes fixed upon her that each was in his way comprehended. She had taken care that each should. For weeks she had used all her story telling power to explain the meanings of the poetry and legendry of the traditional religious carols and some more obscure folk carols. She had brought pictures for them and played records by world famous choirs until they had absorbed the ancient atmosphere to her satisfaction.

"Jack Thompson, I hope your Irish tenor is not feeling out of place tonight. And do you remember how I told you to sing the word 'silent' in your Silent night solo part?"

"Yes, Miss Laurie; I was practicing tonight for the cows." The nervous performers exploded with laughter. Some began to "moo" and someone else announced that the Thompson's bull also had an Irish tenor. Miss Laurie tolerated the outburst; it was a way of releasing tension.

"Lorrain, may I see you a moment?" a girl stepped down from the cluster of sopranos. All evening she had been an object of reverent admiration. She wore a white satin dress that fell in gleaming folds from a closely fitted bodice. The sleeves were loose and gracefully long. The dress and its wearer expressed an attitude of charming innocence suddenly bewildering to Miss Laurie. Lorraine was to be the surprise and climax of the evening and Miss Laurie's triumph. She had discovered the girl's voice, its clear, true tones and unexpected power. She had spent long hours alone with Lorraine, teaching her how to develop and use her voice. Miss Laurie would have her this Christmas and two more, providing she didn't marry that hulking boy she had seen her running around with in town—son of the local drugstore owner. Miss Laurie seldom gave an entire piece for a solo but Lorrain had one solo; she was to sing from the top step.

"Lorraine, you look like an angel," Miss Laurie said in sincere amazement.

"My mother's wedding dress. She cut it up to make this for me since you said I should wear something different," Lorraine murmured in embarrassment.

Miss Laurie, struck by the incongruity, perversely wanted to laugh. This was absurd, a caricature of her own designs. Still, she felt a part of her triumph stealing from her as she stood there. Someone else had been planning, anticipating the occasion. Someone else in the audience would be waiting, perhaps, for the same spiritual reward Miss Laurie coveted: the moment of perfect triumph.

"How do you feel Lorraine? You aren't frightened?" Miss Laurie whispered and her eyes blazed at the girl.

"I don't think so. I want it to be perfect for you and my mother."

"About everyone is seated now, I think; we should begin," Miss Laurie addressed the group. "Does anyone have any questions?" Since there were none, she turned to leave the stage; she stopped once, smiling. "And I wish all of you a Merry Christmas," she whispered again.

When the audience perceived the tall woman walking stiffly across the auditorium to her seat in the front row, several warning hisses sounded and Miss Laurie heard her name breath once or twice. The shabby, velvet curtains parted and jerkily swept across the stage. Miss Laurie sighed. She had forgotten to instruct her stage manager about that. Miss Laurie turned in her seat to observe all faces turned up towards the bright scene on the stage. She wondered if she would recognize Lorraine's mother in the audience but the light was too dim to distinguish individuals. By the time she had brought the pitch pipe to her lips, the hush had fallen.

The program proceeded perfectly and according to plan. The group walked about the steps between songs, stamping their feet and rubbing their hands from imagined cold; Miss Laurie had almost forgotten that detail herself. She relaxed while she listened and closed her eyes, her critical faculties suspended. They were singing with great liveliness tonight, enjoying themselves. Their strong, young voices remembered all she had taught them to feel about the music. Pure spontaneous emotion was there as well as the studied subtlety, for they were beginning to grasp their hold over an audience, the many familiar faces obscured to anonymity beyond the footlights; even Miss Laurie's melted among them.

Miss Laurie heard her proof. The intangible spirit of Christmas rang in her ears. The illusion she worked so brilliantly to create took form and movement. Vision after vision passed swiftly before her eyes. The brave, gallant affirmation of human love and tenderness, the affirmations born to die, the inexhaustible paradox swayed her mind. Miss Laurie's emotions rose in pride and fell back in humility. She knew again the sweetness of hope and of a distant despair.

She opened her eyes to see Lorraine poised on the top step, slender and radiant. Miss Laurie almost forgot to give her the pitch. My Dancing Days, the carol she had always wanted to hear sung the way Lorraine would sing it now. She hadn't been prepared for the girl's transformation; was it all because of the dress? She imagined she saw an answering intelligence in the girl's whole attitude. A kind of mystery hung about Lorraine; something troubling to Miss Laurie in the warm voice. She sang with more assurance than Miss Laurie had thought possible for one with as little experience as Lorraine. She felt herself encompassed by the voice against her will; power and delicacy melted together and Miss Laurie stared fixedly at the white figure. She had never put that quality of sadness in the voice; it was speaking now to Miss Laurie and not only to her—Lorraine was singing to a world beyond the audience. Recognition stirred in Miss Laurie and her mouth fell slightly open. Triumph came but in an altered form. She wanted to tell them all that it wasn't the music; Christmas had something to do with a white satin wedding dress. She would like to know from Lorraine what Christmas was. But Lorraine couldn't tell: she was Christmas; she participated in the sacrifice of innocence to the world. Miss Laurie had never known about Christmas, she realized; she would like to learn now but in the very moment of discovery, she found herself inadequate to make it. "This have I done for my true love". The chorus ended and Lorraine soared into another verse.

June E. Lobdell-Skjervold

# Acknowledgements

Thank you to Olivia Skjervold for transcribing the poems and adapting the manuscripts for publication, and James Maertens for invaluable assistance, insight, proofing, title suggestions and moral support. Thanks also to Kristafer and Stephanie Skjervold, Sara and Mark Paulson, Nathan & Alida Skjervold, Madeline, Julia, Karli & Loretta, Andrew and Paul Skjervold.

# About the Author

*It seems they laugh at poets.....*

*Drawing of June by Phyllis Brussel*

June Lobdell-Skjervold has loved poetry all her life. June attended Reed College in Portland, Oregon and graduated from the University of Minnesota with a B.A. in English Literature. June lives in Shorewood, Minnesota with her beloved cat Pearl less than a mile from her childhood home. June's lifelong appreciation of the natural world is a thread running throughout these poems, and she is an avid environmentalist.

www.ingramcontent.com/pod-product-compliance
Lightning Source LLC
Chambersburg PA
CBHW032008080426
42735CB00007B/547